The SMALCALD ARTICLES

GREAT CHRISTIAN BOOKS
LINDENHURST, NEW YORK

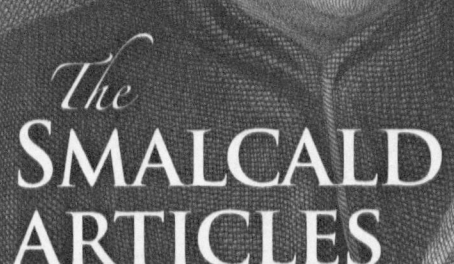

The
SMALCALD
ARTICLES

MARTIN
LUTHER

A GREAT CHRISTIAN BOOKS publication
Great Christian Books is an imprint of Rotolo Media
160 37th Street Lindenhurst, New York 11757
www.GreatChristianBooks.com   (631) 956-0998
email: mail@greatchristianbooks.com
The Smalcald Articles
ISBN 978-1-61010-165-3

Luther, Martin, 1483-1546
The Smalcald Articles / by Martin Luther
p. cm.
A "A Great Christian Book" book
GREAT CHRISTIAN BOOKS an imprint of Rotolo Media
ISBN 978-1-61010-146-2
Dewey Decimal Classifications: 200, 230
Suggested Subject Headings:
1. Religion—Christian literature—Christianity &
Christian theology
2. Christianity—The Bible—Creeds and Confessions
I. Title

Book and cover design for this title are by Michael Rotolo.
Body text is typeset in the Minion typeface by Adobe Inc. and
is quality manufactured in the United States on acid-free paper.
To discuss the publication of your Christian manuscript or out-
of-print book, please contact Great Christian Books.

**MANUFACTURED IN
THE UNITED STATES OF AMERICA**

The Smalcald Articles are Articles of Christian Doctrine which were to have been presented on our part to the Council, if any had been assembled at Mantua or elsewhere, indicating what we could accept or yield, and what we could not.

—Dr. Martin Luther, 1537

Translated by F. Bente and W. H. T. Dau

Preface of
Dr. Martin Luther

Since Pope Paul III convoked a Council last year, to assemble at Mantua about Whitsuntide, and afterwards transferred it from Mantua, so that it is not yet known where he will or can fix it, and we on our part either had to expect that we would be summoned also to the Council or (to fear that we would) be condemned unsummoned, I was directed to compile and collect the articles of our doctrine (in order that it might be plain) in case of deliberation as to what and how far we would be both willing and able to yield to the Papists, and in what points we intended to persevere and abide to the end.

I have accordingly compiled these articles and presented them to our side. They have also been accepted and unanimously confessed by our side, and it has been resolved that, in case the Pope with his adherents should ever be so bold as seriously and in good faith, without lying and cheating, to hold a truly free (legitimate)

Christian Council (as, indeed, he would be in duty bound to do), they be publicly delivered in order to set forth the Confession of our Faith.

But though the Romish court is so dreadfully afraid of a free Christian Council, and shuns the light so shamefully, that it has (entirely) removed, even from those who are on its side, the hope that it will ever permit a free Council, much less that it will itself hold one, whereat, as is just, they (many Papists) are greatly offended and have no little trouble on that account (are disgusted with this negligence of the Pope), since they notice thereby that the Pope would rather see all Christendom perish and all souls damned than suffer either himself or his adherents to be reformed even a little, and his (their) tyranny to be limited, nevertheless I have determined meanwhile to publish these articles in plain print, so that, should I die before there would be a Council (as I fully expect and hope, because the knaves who flee the light and shun the day take such wretched pains to delay and hinder the Council), those who live and remain after me may have my testimony and confession to produce, in addition to the Confession which I have issued previously, whereby up to this time I have abided, and, by God's grace, will abide.

For what shall I say? How shall I complain? I am still living, writing, preaching, and lecturing daily; (and) yet there are found such spiteful men, not only among the adversaries, but also false brethren that profess to be on our side, as dare to cite my writings and doctrine directly against myself, and let me look on and listen, although they know well that I teach otherwise, and as wish to adorn their venom with my labor, and under my name to (deceive and) mislead the poor people. (Good God!) Alas! what first will happen when I am dead?

Indeed, I ought to reply to everything while I am still living. But, again, how can I alone stop all the mouths of the devil? especially of those (as they all are poisoned) who will not hear or notice what we write, but solely exercise themselves with all diligence how they may most shamefully pervert and corrupt our word in every letter. These I let the devil answer, or at last Gods wrath, as they deserve. I often think of the good Gerson who doubts whether anything good should be (written and) published. If it is not done, many souls are neglected who could be delivered: but if it is done, the devil is there with malignant, villainous tongues without number which envenom and pervert everything, so that nevertheless the fruit (the usefulness of the writings) is prevented. Yet what they gain thereby is manifest. For while they have lied so shamefully against us and by means of lies wished to retain the people, God has constantly advanced His work, and been making their following ever smaller and ours greater, and by their lies has caused and still causes them to be brought to shame.

I must tell a story. There was a doctor sent here to Wittenberg from France, who said publicly before us that his king was sure and more than sure, that among us there is no church, no magistrate, no married life, but all live promiscuously as cattle, and each one does as he pleases. Imagine now, how will those who by their writings have instilled such gross lies into the king and other countries as the pure truth, look at us on that day before the judgment-seat of Christ? Christ, the Lord and Judge of us all, knows well that they lie and have (always) lied, His sentence they in turn, must hear; that I know certainly. God convert to repentance those who can be converted! Regarding the rest it will be said, Woe, and, alas! eternally.

But to return to the subject. I verily desire to see a truly Christian Council (assembled some time), in order that many matters and persons might be helped. Not that we need It, for our churches are now, through God's grace, so enlightened and equipped with the pure Word and right use of the Sacraments, with knowledge of the various callings and of right works, that we on our part ask for no Council, and on such points have nothing better to hope or expect from a Council. But we see in the bishoprics everywhere so many parishes vacant and desolate that one's heart would break, and yet neither the bishops nor canons care how the poor people live or die, for whom nevertheless Christ has died, and who are not permitted to hear Him speak with them as the true Shepherd with His sheep. This causes me to shudder and fear that at some time He may send a council of angels upon Germany utterly destroying us, like Sodom and Gomorrah, because we so wantonly mock Him with the Council.

Besides such necessary ecclesiastical affairs, there would be also in the political estate innumerable matters of great importance to improve. There is the disagreement between the princes and the states; usury and avarice have burst in like a flood, and have become lawful (are defended with a show of right);

wantonness, lewdness, extravagance in dress, gluttony, gambling, idle display, with all kinds of bad habits and wickedness, insubordination of subjects, of domestics and laborers of every trade, also the exactions (and most exorbitant selling prices) of the peasants (and who can enumerate all?) have so increased that they cannot be rectified by ten Councils and twenty Diets. If such chief matters of the spiritual and worldly estates as are contrary to God would be considered in the Council, they would have all hands so full that the child's play and absurdity of long gowns (official insignia), large tonsures, broad cinctures (or sashes), bishops' or cardinals' hats or maces, and like jugglery would in the mean time be forgotten. If we first had performed God's command and order in the spiritual and secular estate we would find time enough to reform food, clothing, tonsures, and surplices. But if we want to swallow such camels, and, instead, strain at gnats, let the beams stand and judge the motes, we also might indeed be satisfied with the Council.

Therefore I have presented few articles; for we have without this so many commands of God to observe in the Church, the state and the family that we can never fulfil them. What, then, is the use, or what does it profit that many decrees and statutes thereon are made in the Council, especially when these chief matters commanded of God are neither regarded nor observed? Just as though He were bound to honor our jugglery as a reward of our treading His solemn commandments under foot. But our sins weigh upon us and cause God not to be gracious to us; for we do not repent, and, besides, wish to defend every abomination.

O Lord Jesus Christ, do Thou Thyself convoke a Council, and deliver Thy servants by Thy glorious advent! The Pope and his adherents are done for; they will have none of Thee. Do Thou, then, help us, who are poor and needy, who sigh to Thee, and beseech Thee earnestly, according to the grace which Thou hast given us, through Thy Holy Ghost who liveth and reigneth with Thee and the Father, blessed forever. Amen.

THE FIRST PART

Treats of the Sublime Articles Concerning the Divine Majesty, as:

I. That Father, Son, and Holy Ghost, three distinct persons in one divine essence and nature, are one God, who has created heaven and earth.

II. That the Father is begotten of no one; the Son of the Father; the Holy Ghost proceeds from Father and Son.

III. That not the Father nor the Holy Ghost but the Son became man.

IV. That the Son became man in this manner, that He was conceived, without the cooperation of man, by the Holy Ghost, and was born of the pure, holy (and always) Virgin Mary. Afterwards He suffered, died, was buried, descended to hell, rose from the dead, ascended to heaven, sits at the right hand of God, will come to judge the quick and the dead, etc. as the Creed of the Apostles, as well as that of St. Athanasius, and the Catechism in common use for children, teach.

Concerning these articles there is no contention or dispute, since we on both sides confess them. Therefore it is not necessary now to treat further of them.

THE SECOND PART

Treats of the Articles which Refer to the Office and Work of Jesus Christ, or Our Redemption.

Article I: Of Christ

The first and chief article is this,

That Jesus Christ, our God and Lord, died for our sins, and was raised again for our justification, Rom. 4:25.

And He alone is the Lamb of God which taketh away the sins of the world, John 1:29; and God has laid upon Him the iniquities of us all, Is. 53:6.

Likewise: All have sinned and are justified without merit (freely, and without their own works or merits) by His grace, through the redemption that is in Christ Jesus, in His blood, Rom. 3:23 f.

Now, since it is necessary to believe this, and it cannot be otherwise acquired or apprehended by any work, law, or merit, it is clear and certain that this faith alone justifies us as St. Paul says, Rom. 3:28: For we conclude that a man is justified by faith, without the deeds of the Law. Likewise v. 26: That He might be just, and the Justifier of him which believeth in Christ.

Of this article nothing can be yielded or surrendered (nor can anything be granted or permitted contrary to the same), even though heaven and earth, and whatever will not abide, should sink to ruin. For there is none other name under heaven, given among men whereby we must be saved, says Peter, Acts 4:12. And with His stripes we are healed, Is. 53:5. And upon this article all things depend which we teach and practice in opposition to the Pope, the devil, and the (whole) world. Therefore, we must be sure concerning this doctrine, and not doubt; for otherwise all is lost, and the Pope and devil and all things gain the victory and suit over us.

Article II: Of the Mass

That the Mass in the Papacy must be the greatest and most horrible abomination, as it directly and powerfully conflicts with this chief article, and yet above and before all other popish idolatries it has been the chief and most specious. For it has been held that this sacrifice or work of the Mass, even though it be rendered by a wicked (and abandoned) scoundrel, frees men from sins, both in this life and also in purgatory, while only the Lamb of God shall and must do this, as has been said above. Of this article nothing is to be surrendered or conceded, because the first article does not allow it.

If, perchance, there were reasonable Papists we might speak moderately and in a friendly way, thus: first, why they so rigidly uphold the Mass. For it is but a pure invention of men, and has not been commanded by God; and every invention of man we may (safely) discard, as Christ declares, Matt. 15:9: In vain do they worship Me, teaching for doctrines the commandments of men.

Secondly. It is an unnecessary thing, which can be omitted without sin and danger.

Thirdly. The Sacrament can be received in a better and more blessed way (more acceptable to God), (yea, the only blessed way), according to the institution of Christ. Why, then, do they drive the world to woe and (extreme) misery on account of a fictitious, unnecessary matter, which can be well obtained in another and more blessed way?

Let (care be taken that) it be publicly preached to the people that the Mass as men's twaddle (commentitious affair or human figment) can be omitted without sin, and that no one will be condemned who does not observe it, but that he can be saved in a better way without the Mass. I wager (Thus it will come to pass) that the Mass will then collapse of itself, not only among the insane (rude) common people, but also among all pious, Christian, reasonable, God-fearing hearts; and that the more, when they would hear that the Mass is a (very) dangerous thing, fabricated and invented without the will and Word of God.

Fourthly. Since such innumerable and unspeakable abuses have arisen in the whole world from the buying and selling of masses, the Mass should by right be relinquished, if for no other purpose than to prevent abuses, even though in itself it had something advantageous and good. How much more ought we to relinquish it, so as to prevent (escape) forever these horrible abuses, since it is altogether unnecessary, useless, and dangerous, and we can obtain everything by a more necessary, profitable, and certain way without the Mass.

Fifthly. But since the Mass is nothing else and

can be nothing else (as the Canon and all books declare), than a work of men (even of wicked scoundrels), by which one attempts to reconcile himself and others to God, and to obtain and merit the remission of sins and grace (for thus the Mass is observed when it is observed at the very best; otherwise what purpose would it serve?), for this very reason it must and should (certainly) be condemned and rejected. For this directly conflicts with the chief article, which says that it is not a wicked or a godly hireling of the Mass with his own work, but the Lamb of God and the Son of God, that taketh away our sins.

But if any one should advance the pretext that as an act of devotion he wishes to administer the Sacrament, or Communion, to himself, he is not in earnest (he would commit a great mistake, and would not be speaking seriously and sincerely). For if he wishes to commune in sincerity, the surest and best way for him is in the Sacrament administered according to Christ's institution. But that one administer communion to himself is a human notion, uncertain, unnecessary, yea, even prohibited. And he does not know what he is doing, because without the Word of God he obeys a false human opinion and invention. So, too, it is not right (even though the matter were otherwise correct) for one to use the common Sacrament of (belonging to) the Church according to his own private devotion, and without God's Word and apart from the communion of the Church to trifle therewith.

This article concerning the Mass will be the whole business of the Council. (The Council will perspire most over, and be occupied with this article concerning the Mass.) For if it were (although it would be) possible for them to concede to us all the other articles, yet they could not concede this. As Campegius said at Augsburg that he would be torn to pieces before he would relinquish the Mass, so, by the help of God, I, too, would suffer myself to be reduced to ashes before I would allow a hireling of the Mass, be he good or bad, to be made equal to Christ Jesus, my Lord and Savior, or to be exalted above Him. Thus we are and remain eternally separated and opposed to one another. They feel well enough that when the Mass falls, the Papacy lies in ruins. Before they will permit this to occur, they will put us all to death if they can.

In addition to all this, this dragon's tail, (I mean) the Mass, has begotten a numerous vermin-brood of manifold idolatries.

First, purgatory. Here they carried their trade into purgatory by masses for souls, and vigils, and weekly, monthly, and yearly celebrations of obsequies, and finally by the Common Week and All Souls Day, by soul-baths so that the Mass is used almost alone for the dead, although Christ has instituted the Sacrament alone for the living. Therefore purgatory, and every solemnity, rite, and commerce connected with it, is to be regarded as nothing but a specter of the devil. For it conflicts with the chief article (which teaches) that only Christ, and not the works of men, are to help (set free) souls. Not to mention the fact that nothing has been (divinely) commanded or enjoined upon us concerning the dead. Therefore all this may be safely omitted, even if it were no error and idolatry.

The Papists quote here Augustine and some of the Fathers who are said to have written concerning purgatory, and they think that we do not understand for what purpose and to what end they spoke as they did. St. Augustine does not write that there is a purgatory nor has he a testimony of Scripture to constrain him thereto, but he leaves it in doubt whether there is one, and says that his mother asked to be remembered at the altar or Sacrament. Now, all this is indeed nothing but the devotion of men, and that, too, of individuals, and does not establish an article of faith, which is the prerogative of God alone.

Our Papists, however, cite such statements (opinions) of men in order that men should believe in their horrible, blasphemous, and cursed traffic in masses for souls in purgatory (or in sacrifices for the dead and oblations), etc. But they will never prove these things from Augustine. Now, when they have abolished the traffic in masses for purgatory, of which Augustine never dreamt, we will then discuss with them whether the expressions of Augustine without Scripture (being without the warrant of the Word) are to be admitted, and whether the dead should be remembered at the Eucharist. For it will not do to frame articles of faith from the works or words of the holy Fathers; other-wise their kind of fare, of garments, of house, etc., would have to become an article of faith, as was done with relies. (We have, however, another rule, namely) The rule is: The Word of God shall establish articles of faith, and no one else, not even an angel.

Secondly. From this it has followed that evil spirits have perpetrated much knavery (exercised their malice) by appearing as the souls of the departed, and with unspeakable (horrible) lies and tricks demanded masses, vigils, pilgrimages, and other alms. All of which we had to receive as articles of faith, and to live accordingly; and the Pope confirmed these things, as also the Mass and all other abominations. Here, too, there is no (cannot and must not be any) yielding or surrendering.

Thirdly. (Hence arose) the pilgrimages. Here, too, masses, the remission of sins and the grace of God were sought, for the Mass controlled everything. Now it is indeed certain that such pilgrimages, without the Word of God, have not been commanded us, neither are they necessary, since we can have these things (the soul can be cared for) in a better way, and can omit these pilgrimages without any sin and danger. Why therefore do they leave at home (desert) their own parish (their called ministers, their parishes), the Word of God, wives, children, etc., who are ordained and (attention to whom is necessary and has been) commanded, and run after these unnecessary, uncertain, pernicious will-o'-the-wisps of the devil (and errors)? Unless the devil was riding (made insane) the Pope, causing him to praise and establish these practices, whereby the people again and again revolted from Christ to their own works, and became idolaters, which is worst of all; moreover, it is neither necessary nor commanded, but is senseless and doubtful, and besides harmful. Hence here, too, there can be no yielding or surrendering (to yield or concede anything here is not lawful), etc. And let this be preached, that such pilgrimages are not necessary, but dangerous; and then see what will become of them. (For thus they will perish of their own accord.)

Fourthly. Fraternities (or societies), in which cloisters, chapters, vicars have assigned and communicated (by a legal contract and sale) all masses and good works, etc., both for the living and the dead. This is not only altogether a human bauble, without the Word of God, entirely unnecessary and not commanded, but also contrary to the chief article, Of Redemption. Therefore it is in no way to be tolerated.

Fifthly. The relics, in which there are found so many falsehoods and tomfooleries concerning the bones of dogs and horses, that even the devil has laughed at such rascalities, ought long ago to have been condemned, even though there were some good in them; and so much the more because they are without the Word of God; being neither commanded nor counseled, they are an entirely unnecessary and useless thing. But the worst is that (they have imagined that) these relics had to work indulgence and the forgiveness of sins (and have revered them) as a good work and service of God, like the Mass, etc.

Sixthly. Here belong the precious indulgences granted (but only for money) both to the living and the dead, by which the miserable (sacrilegious and accursed) Judas, or Pope, has sold the merit of Christ, together with the superfluous merits of all saints and of the entire Church, etc. All these things (and every single one of them) are not to be borne, and are not only without the Word of God, without necessity, not commanded, but are against the chief article. For the merit of Christ is (apprehended and) obtained not by our works or pence, but from grace through faith, without money and merit; and is offered (and presented) not through the power of the Pope, but through the preaching of God's Word.

Of the Invocation of Saints

The invocation of saints is also one of the abuses of Antichrist conflicting with the chief article, and destroys the knowledge of Christ.

Neither is it commanded nor counseled, nor
has it any example (or testimony) in Scripture,
and even though it were a precious thing, as
it is not (while, on the contrary, it is a most
harmful thing), in Christ we have everything a
thousandfold better (and surer, so that we are
not in need of calling upon the saints).

And although the angels in heaven pray for
us (as Christ Himself also does), as also do the
saints on earth, and perhaps also in heaven, yet
it does not follow thence that we should invoke
and adore the angels and saints, and fast, hold
festivals, celebrate Mass in their honor, make
offerings, and establish churches, altars, divine
worship, and in still other ways serve them, and
regard them as helpers in need (as patrons and
intercessors), and divide among them all kinds
of help, and ascribe to each one a particular form
of assistance, as the Papists teach and do. For
this is idolatry, and such honor belongs alone
to God. For as a Christian and saint upon earth
you can pray for me, not only in one, but in
many necessities. But for this reason I am not
obliged to adore and invoke you, and celebrate
festivals, fast, make oblations, hold masses for
your honor (and worship), and put my faith in
you for my salvation. I can in other ways indeed

honor, love, and thank you in Christ. If now such idolatrous honor were withdrawn from angels and departed saints, the remaining honor would be without harm and would quickly be forgotten. For when advantage and assistance, both bodily and spiritual, are no more to be expected, the saints will not be troubled (the worship of the saints will soon vanish), neither in their graves nor in heaven. For without a reward or out of pure love no one will much remember, or esteem, or honor them (bestow on them divine honor).

In short, the Mass itself and anything that proceeds from it, and anything that is attached to it, we cannot tolerate, but must condemn, in order that we may retain the holy Sacrament pure and certain, according to the institution of Christ, employed and received through faith.

Article III:
Of Chapters and Cloisters

That chapters and cloisters (colleges of canons and communistic dwellings), which were formerly founded with the good intention (of our forefathers) to educate learned men and chaste (and modest) women, ought again to be turned to such use, in order that pastors, preachers, and other ministers of the churches may be had, and likewise other necessary persons (fitted) for (the political administration of) the secular government (or for the commonwealth) in cities and countries, and well-educated, maidens for mothers and housekeepers, etc.

If they will not serve this purpose, it is better that they be abandoned or razed, rather than (continued and), with their blasphemous services invented by men, regarded as something better than the ordinary Christian life and the offices and callings ordained by God. For all this also is contrary to the first chief article concerning the redemption made through Jesus Christ. Add to this that (like all other human inventions) these have neither been commanded; they are needless and useless, and, besides, afford occasion for dangerous and vain labor (dangerous annoyances and fruitless worship), such services as the prophets call Aven, i.e., pain and labor.

Article IV: Of the Papacy

That the Pope is not, according to divine law or according to the Word of God the head of all Christendom (for this (name) belongs to One only, whose name is Jesus Christ), but is only the bishop and pastor of the Church at Rome, and of those who voluntarily or through a human creature (that is, a political magistrate) have attached themselves to him, to be Christians, not under him as a lord, but with him as brethren (colleagues) and comrades, as the ancient councils and the age of St. Cyprian show.

But today none of the bishops dare to address the Pope as brother as was done at that time (in the age of Cyprian); but they must call him most gracious lord, even though they be kings or emperors. This (Such arrogance) we will not, cannot, must not take upon our conscience (with a good conscience approve). Let him, however, who will do it, do so without us (at his own risk).

Hence it follows that all things which the Pope, from a power so false, mischievous, blasphemous, and arrogant, has done and undertaken, have been and still are purely diabolical affairs and transactions (with the exception of such things as pertain to the secular government, where God often permits much good to be effected for a people, even through a tyrant and (faithless) scoundrel) for the ruin of the entire holy (catholic or) Christian Church (so far as it is in his power) and for the destruction of the first and chief article concerning the redemption made through Jesus Christ.

For all his bulls and books are extant, in which he roars like a lion (as the angel in Rev. 12 depicts him), (crying out) that no Christian can be saved unless he obeys him and is subject to him in all things that he wishes, that he says, and that he does. All of which amounts to nothing less than saying: Although you believe in Christ, and have in Him (alone) everything that is necessary to salvation, yet it is nothing and all in vain unless you regard (have and worship) me as your god, and be subject and obedient to me. And yet it is manifest that the holy Church has been without the Pope for at least more than five hundred years, and that even to the present day the churches of the Greeks and of many other languages neither have been nor are yet under the Pope. Besides, as often remarked, it is a human figment which is not commanded, and is unnecessary and useless; for the holy Christian (or catholic) Church can exist very well without such a head, and it would certainly have remained better (purer, and its career would have been more prosperous) if such a head had not been raised up by the devil. And the Papacy is also of no use in the Church, because it exercises no Christian office; and therefore it is necessary for the Church to continue and to exist without the Pope.

And supposing that the Pope would yield this point, so as not to be supreme by divine right or from Gods command, but that we must have (there must be elected) a (certain) head, to whom all the rest adhere (as their support) in order that the (concord and) unity of Christians may be preserved against sects and heretics, and that such a head were chosen by men, and that it were placed within the choice and power of men to change or remove this head, just as the Council of Constance adopted nearly this course with reference to the Popes, deposing three and electing a fourth; supposing, I say, that the Pope and See at Rome would yield and accept this (which, nevertheless, is impossible; for thus he would have to suffer his entire realm and estate to be overthrown and destroyed, with all his rights and books, a thing which, to speak in few words, he cannot do), nevertheless, even in this way Christianity would not be helped, but many more sects would arise than before.

For since men would have to be subject to this head, not from God's command, but from their personal good pleasure, it would easily and in a short time be despised, and at last retain no member; neither would it have to be forever confined to Rome or any other place, but it might be wherever and in whatever church God would grant a man fit for the (taking upon him such a great) office. Oh, the complicated and confused state of affairs (perplexity) that would result!

Therefore the Church can never be better governed and preserved than if we all live under one head, Christ, and all the bishops equal in office (although they be unequal in gifts), be diligently joined in unity of doctrine, faith, Sacraments, prayer, and works of love, etc., as St. Jerome writes that the priests at Alexandria together and in common governed the churches, as did also the apostles, and afterwards all bishops throughout all Christendom, until the Pope raised his head above all.

This teaching shows forcefully that the Pope is the very Antichrist, who has exalted himself above, and opposed himself against Christ because he will not permit Christians to be saved without his power, which, nevertheless, is nothing, and is neither ordained nor commanded by God. This is, properly speaking to exalt himself above all that is called God as Paul says, 2 Thess. 2:4. Even the Turks or the Tartars, great enemies of Christians as they are, do not do this, but they allow whoever wishes to believe in Christ, and take bodily tribute and obedience from Christians.

The Pope, however, prohibits this faith, saying that to be saved a person must obey him. This we are unwilling to do, even though on this account we must die in God s name. This all proceeds from the fact that the Pope has wished to be called the supreme head of the Christian Church by divine right. Accordingly he had to make himself equal and superior to Christ, and had to cause himself to be proclaimed the head and then the lord of the Church, and finally of the whole world, and simply God on earth, until he has dared to issue commands even to the angels in heaven. And when we distinguish the Pope s teaching from, or measure and hold it against, Holy Scripture, it is found (it appears plainly) that the Pope s teaching, where it is best, has been taken from the imperial and heathen law and treats of political matters and decisions or rights, as the Decretals show; furthermore, it teaches of ceremonies concerning churches, garments, food, persons and (similar) puerile, theatrical and comical things without measure, but in all these things nothing at all of Christ, faith, and the commandments of God. Lastly, it is nothing else than the devil himself, because above and against God he urges (and disseminates) his (papal) falsehoods concerning masses, purgatory, the monastic life, one's own works and (fictitious) divine worship (for this is the very Papacy (upon each of which the Papacy is altogether founded and is standing)), and condemns, murders and tortures all Christians who do not exalt and honor these abominations (of the Pope) above all things. Therefore, just as little as we can worship the devil himself as Lord and God, we can endure his apostle, the Pope, or Antichrist, in his rule as head or lord. For to lie and to kill, and to destroy body and soul eternally, that is wherein his papal government really consists, as I have very clearly shown in many books.

In these four articles they will have enough to condemn in the Council. For they cannot and will not concede us even the least point in one of these articles. Of this we should be certain, and animate ourselves with (be forewarned and made firm in) the hope that Christ, our Lord, has attacked His adversary, and he will press the attack home (pursue and destroy him) both by His Spirit and coming. Amen.

For in the Council we will stand not before the Emperor or the political magistrate, as at Augsburg (where the Emperor published a most gracious edict, and caused matters to be heard kindly (and dispassionately)), but (we will appear) before the Pope and devil himself, who intends to listen to nothing, but merely (when the case has been publicly announced) to condemn, to murder and to force us to idolatry. Therefore we ought not here to kiss his feet, or to say: Thou art my gracious lord, but as the angel in Zechariah 3:2 said to Satan: The Lord rebuke thee, O Satan.

THE THIRD PART

Concerning the following articles we may (will be able to) treat with learned and reasonable men, or among ourselves. The Pope and his (the Papal) government do not care much about these. For with them conscience is nothing, but money, (glory) honors, power are (to them) everything.

I. Of Sin

Here we must confess, as Paul says in Rom. 5:11, that sin originated (and entered the world) from one man Adam, by whose disobedience all men were made sinners, (and) subject to death and the devil. This is called original or capital sin.

The fruits of this sin are afterwards the evil deeds which are forbidden in the Ten Commandments, such as (distrust) unbelief, false faith, idolatry, to be without the fear of God, presumption (recklessness), despair, blindness (or complete loss of sight), and, in short not to know or regard God; furthermore to lie, to swear by (to abuse) God's name (to swear falsely), not to pray, not to call upon God, not to regard (to despise or neglect) God's Word, to be disobedient to parents, to murder, to be unchaste, to steal, to deceive, etc.

This hereditary sin is so deep and (horrible) a corruption of nature that no reason can understand it, but it must be (learned and) believed from the revelation of Scriptures, Ps. 51:5; Rom. 6:12 ff.; Ex. 33:3; Gen. 3:7 ff. Hence, it is nothing but error and blindness in regard to this article what the scholastic doctors have taught, namely:

That since the fall of Adam the natural powers of man have remained entire and incorrupt, and that man by nature has a right reason and a good will; which things the philosophers teach.

Again that man has a free will to do good and omit evil, and, conversely, to omit good and do evil.

Again, that man by his natural powers can observe and keep (do) all the commands of God.

Again, that, by his natural powers, man can love God above all things and his neighbor as himself.

Again, if a man does as much as is in him,

God certainly grants him His grace.

Again, if he wishes to go to the Sacrament, there is no need of a good intention to do good, but it is sufficient if he has not a wicked purpose to commit sin; so entirely good is his nature and so efficacious the Sacrament.

(Again,) that it is not founded upon Scripture that for a good work the Holy Ghost with His grace is necessary.

Such and many similar things have arisen from want of understanding and ignorance as regards both this sin and Christ, our Savior and they are truly heathen dogmas, which we cannot endure. For if this teaching were right (approved), then Christ has died in vain, since there is in man no defect nor sin for which he should have died; or He would have died only for the body, not for the soul, inasmuch as the soul is (entirely) sound, and the body only is subject to death.

II. Of the Law

Here we hold that the Law was given by God, first, to restrain sin by threats and the dread of punishment, and by the promise and offer of grace and benefit. But all this miscarried on account of the wickedness which sin has wrought in man. For thereby a part (some) were rendered worse, those, namely, who are hostile to (hate) the Law, because it forbids what they like to do, and enjoins what they do not like to do. Therefore, wherever they can escape (if they were not restrained by) punishment, they (would) do more against the Law than before. These, then, are the rude and wicked (unbridled and secure) men, who do evil wherever they (notice that they) have the opportunity.

The rest become blind and arrogant (are smitten with arrogance and blindness), and (insolently) conceive the opinion that they observe and can observe the Law by their own powers, as has been said above concerning the scholastic theologians; thence come the hypocrites and (self-righteous or) false saints.

But the chief office or force of the Law is that it reveal original sin with all its fruits, and show man how very low his nature has fallen, and has become (fundamentally and) utterly corrupted; as the Law must tell man that he has no God nor regards (cares for) God, and worships other gods, a matter which before and without the Law he would not have believed. In this way he becomes terrified, is humbled, desponds, despairs, and anxiously desires aid, but sees no escape; he begins to be an enemy of (enraged at) God, and to murmur, etc. This is what Paul says, Rom. 4:15: The Law worketh wrath. And Rom. 5:20: Sin is increased by the Law. (The Law entered that the offense might abound.)

III. Of Repentance

This office (of the Law) the New Testament retains and urges, as St. Paul, Rom. 1:18 does, saying: The wrath of God is revealed from heaven against all ungodliness and unrighteousness of men. Again, v. 3:19: All the world is guilty before God. No man is righteous before Him. And Christ says, John 16:8: The Holy Ghost will reprove the world of sin.

This, then, is the thunderbolt of God by which He strikes in a heap (hurls to the ground) both manifest sinners and false saints (hypocrites), and suffers no one to be in the right (declares no one righteous), but drives them all together to terror and despair. This is the hammer, as Jeremiah says, v. 23:29: Is not My Word like a hammer that breaketh the rock in pieces? This is not activa contritio or manufactured repentance, but passiva contritio (torture of conscience), true sorrow of heart, suffering and sensation of death.

This, then, is what it means to begin true repentance; and here man must hear such a sentence as this: You are all of no account, whether you be manifest sinners or saints (in your own opinion); you all must become different and do otherwise than you now are and are doing (no matter what sort of people you are), whether you are as great, wise, powerful, and holy as you may. Here no one is (righteous, holy), godly, etc.

But to this office the New Testament immediately adds the consolatory promise of grace through the Gospel, which must be believed, as Christ declares, Mark 1,15: Repent and believe the Gospel, i.e., become different and do otherwise, and believe My promise. And John, preceding Him, is called a preacher of repentance, however, for the remission of sins, i.e., John was to accuse all, and convict them of being sinners, that they might know what they were before God, and might acknowledge that they were lost men, and might thus be prepared for the Lord, to receive grace, and to expect and accept from Him the remission of sins. Thus also Christ Himself says, Luke 24:47: Repentance and remission of sins must be preached in My name among all nations.

But whenever the Law alone, without the Gospel being added exercises this its office there is (nothing else than) death and hell, and man must despair, like Saul and Judas; as St. Paul, Rom. 7:10, says: Through sin the Law killeth. On the other hand, the Gospel brings consolation and remission not only in one way, but through the word and Sacraments, and the like, as we shall hear afterward in order that (thus) there is with the Lord plenteous redemption, as Ps. 130:7 says against the dreadful captivity of sin.

However, we must now contrast the false repentance of the sophists with true repentance, in order that both may be the better understood.

Of the False Repentance of the Papists

It was impossible that they should teach correctly concerning repentance, since they did not (rightly) know the real sins (the real sin). For, as has been shown above, they do not believe aright concerning original sin, but say that the natural powers of man have remained (entirely) unimpaired and incorrupt; that reason can teach aright, and the will can in accordance therewith do aright (perform those things which are taught), that God certainly bestows His grace when a man does as much as is in him, according to his free will.

It had to follow thence (from this dogma) that they did (must do) penance only for actual sins such as wicked thoughts to which a person yields (for wicked emotion (concupiscence, vicious feelings, and inclinations), lust and improper dispositions (according to them) are not sins), and for wicked words and wicked deeds, which free will could readily have omitted.

And of such repentance they fix three parts contrition, confession, and satisfaction, with this (magnificent) consolation and promise added: If man truly repent, (feel remorse,) confess, render satisfaction, he thereby would have merited forgiveness, and paid for his sins before God (atoned for his sins and obtained a plenary redemption). Thus in repentance they instructed men to repose confidence in their own works. Hence the expression originated, which was employed in the pulpit when public absolution was announced to the people: Prolong O God, my life, until I shall make satisfaction for my sins and amend my life.

There was here (profound silence and) no mention of Christ nor faith; but men hoped by their own works to overcome and blot out sins before God. And with this intention we became priests and monks, that we might array ourselves against sin.

As to contrition, this is the way it was done: Since no one could remember all his sins (especially as committed through an entire year), they inserted this provision, namely, that if an unknown sin should be remembered later (if the remembrance of a concealed sin should perhaps return), this also must be repented of and confessed etc. Meanwhile they were (the person was) commended to the grace of God.

Moreover, since no one could know how great the contrition ought to be in order to be sufficient before God, they gave this consolation: He who could not have contrition, at least ought to have attrition, which I may call half a contrition or the beginning of contrition, for they have themselves understood neither of these terms nor do they understand them now, as little as I. Such attrition was reckoned as contrition when a person went to confession.

And when it happened that any one said that he could not have contrition nor lament his sins (as might have occurred in illicit love or the desire for revenge, etc.), they asked whether he did not wish or desire to have contrition (lament). When one would reply Yes (for who, save the devil himself, would here say No?), they accepted this as contrition, and forgave him his sins on account of this good work of his (which they adorned with the name of contrition). Here they cited the example of St. Bernard, etc.

Here we see how blind reason, in matters pertaining to God, gropes about, and, according to its own imagination, seeks for consolation in its own works, and cannot think of (entirely forgets) Christ and faith. But if it be (clearly) viewed in the light, this contrition is a manufactured and fictitious thought (or imagination), derived from man's own powers, without faith and without the knowledge of Christ. And in it the poor sinner, when he reflected upon his own lust and desire for revenge, would sometimes (perhaps) have laughed rather than wept (either laughed or wept, rather than to think of something else), except such as either had been truly struck by (the lightning of) the Law, or had been vainly vexed by the devil with a sorrowful spirit. Otherwise (with the exception of these persons) such contrition was certainly mere hypocrisy, and did not mortify the lust for sins (flames of sin); for they had to grieve, while they would rather have continued to sin, if it had been free to them.

As regards confession, the procedure was this: Every one had (was enjoined) to enumerate all his sins (which is an impossible thing). This was a great torment. From such as he had forgotten (But if any one had forgotten some sins) he would be absolved on the condition that, if they would occur to him, he must still confess them. In this way he could never know whether he had made a sufficiently pure confession (perfectly and correctly), or when confessing would ever have an end. Yet he was pointed to his own works, and comforted thus: The more fully (sincerely and frankly) one confesses, and the more he humiliates himself and debases himself before the priest, the sooner and better he renders satisfaction for his sins; for such humility certainly would earn grace before God.

Here, too, there was no faith nor Christ, and the virtue of the absolution was not declared to him, but upon his enumeration of sins and his self-abasement depended his consolation. What torture, rascality, and idolatry such confession has produced is more than can be related.

As to satisfaction, this is by far the most involved (perplexing) part of all. For no man could know how much to render for a single sin, not to say how much for all. Here they have resorted to the device of imposing a small satisfaction, which could indeed be rendered, as five Paternosters, a day's fast, etc.; for the rest (that was lacking) of the (in their) repentance they were directed to purgatory.

Here, too, there was nothing but anguish and (extreme) misery. (For) some thought that they would never get out of purgatory, because, according to the old canons seven years' repentance is required for a single mortal sin. Nevertheless, confidence was placed upon our work of satisfaction, and if the satisfaction could have been perfect, confidence would have been placed in it entirely, and neither faith nor Christ would have been of use. But this confidence was impossible. For although any one had done penance in that way for a hundred years, he would still not have known whether he had finished his penance. That meant forever to do penance and never to come to repentance.

Here now the Holy See at Rome, coming to the aid of the poor Church, invented indulgences, whereby it forgave and remitted (expiation or) satisfaction, first, for a single instance, for seven years, for a hundred years and distributed them among the cardinals and bishops, so that one could grant indulgence for a hundred years and another for a hundred days. But he reserved to himself alone the power to remit the entire satisfaction.

Now, since this began to yield money, and the traffic in bulls became profitable he devised the golden jubilee year (a truly goldbearing year), and fixed it at Rome. He called this the remission of all punishment and guilt. Then the people came running, because every one would fain have been freed from this grievous, unbearable burden. This meant to find (dig up) and raise the treasures of the earth. Immediately the Pope pressed still further, and multiplied the golden years one upon another. But the more he devoured money, the wider grew his maw.

Later, therefore, he issued them (those golden years of his) by his legates (everywhere) to the countries, until all churches and houses were full of the Golden Year. At last he also made an inroad into purgatory among the dead, first, by founding masses and vigils, afterwards, by indulgences and the Golden Year, and finally souls became so cheap that he released one for a farthing.

But all this, too, was of no avail. For although the Pope taught men to depend upon, and trust in, these indulgences (for salvation), yet he rendered the (whole) matter again uncertain. For in his bulls he declares: Whoever would share in the indulgences or a Golden Year must be contrite, and have confessed, and pay money. Now, we have heard above that this contrition and confession are with them uncertain and hypocrisy. Likewise, also no one knew what soul was in purgatory, and if some were therein, no one knew which had properly repented and confessed. Thus he took the precious money (the Pope snatched up the holy pence), and comforted them meanwhile with (led them to confidence in) his power and indulgence, and (then again led them away from that and) directed them again to their uncertain work.

If, now (although), there were some who did not believe (acknowledge) themselves guilty of such actual sins in (committed by) thoughts, words, and works,—as I, and such as I, in monasteries and chapters (fraternities or colleges of priests), wished to be monks and priests, and by fasting, watching, praying, saying Mass, coarse garments, and hard beds, etc., fought against (strove to resist) evil thoughts, and in full earnest and with force wanted to be holy, and yet the hereditary, inborn evil sometimes did in sleep what it is wont to do (as also St. Augustine and

Jerome among others confess),—still each one held the other in esteem, so that some, according to our teaching, were regarded as holy, without sin and full of good works, so much so that with this mind we would communicate and sell our good works to others, as being superfluous to us for heaven. This is indeed true, and seals, letters, and instances (that this happened) are at hand.

(When there were such, I say) These did not need repentance. For of what would they repent, since they had not indulged wicked thoughts? What would they confess (concerning words not uttered), since they had avoided words? For what should they render satisfaction, since they were so guiltless of any deed that they could even sell their superfluous righteousness to other poor sinners? Such saints were also the Pharisees and scribes in the time of Christ.

Here comes the fiery angel, St. John (Rev. 10), the true preacher of (true) repentance, and with one (thunderclap and) bolt hurls both (those selling and those buying works) on one heap, and says: Repent! Matt. 3:2. Now, the former (the poor wretches) imagine: Why, we have repented! The latter (the rest) say: We need no repentance. John says: Repent ye, both of you, for ye are false penitents; so are these (the rest) false saints (or hypocrites), and all of you on either side need the forgiveness of sins, because neither of you know what true sin is not to say anything about your duty to repent of it and shun it. For no one of you is good; you are full of unbelief, stupidity, and ignorance of God and God's will. For here He is present of whose fulness have all we received, and grace for grace, John 1:16, and without Him no man can be just before God. Therefore, if you wish to repent, repent aright—your penance will not accomplish anything (is nothing). And you hypocrites, who do not need repentance, you serpents' brood, who has assured you that you will escape the wrath to come? etc. Matt. 3:7; Luke 3:7.

In the same way Paul also preaches, Rom. 3:10-12: There is none righteous, there is none that understandeth, there is none that seeketh after God, there is none that doeth good, no not one; they are all gone out of the way; they are together become unprofitable. And Acts 17:30: God now commandeth all men everywhere to repent. "All men," he says; no one excepted who is a man. This repentance teaches us to discern sin, namely, that we are altogether lost, and that there is nothing good in us from head to foot (both within and without), and that we must absolutely become new and other men.

This repentance is not piecemeal (partial) and beggarly (fragmentary), like that which does penance for actual sins, nor is it uncertain like that. For it does not debate what is or is not sin, but hurls everything on a heap, and says: All in us is nothing but sin (affirms that, with respect to us, all is simply sin (and there is nothing in us that is not sin and guilt)). What is the use of (For why do we wish) investigating, dividing, or distinguishing a long time? For this reason, too, this contrition is not (doubtful or) uncertain. For there is nothing left with which we can think of any good thing to pay for sin, but there is only a sure despairing concerning all that we are, think, speak, or do (all hope must be cast aside in respect of everything), etc.

In like manner confession, too, cannot be false, uncertain, or piecemeal (mutilated or fragmentary). For he who confesses that all in him is nothing but sin comprehends all sins excludes none, forgets none. Neither can the satisfaction be uncertain, because it is not our uncertain, sinful work, but it is the suffering and blood of the (spotless and) innocent Lamb of God who taketh away the sin of the world.

Of this repentance John preaches, and afterwards Christ in the Gospel, and we also. By this (preaching of) repentance we dash to the ground the Pope and everything that is built upon our good works. For all is built upon a rotten and vain foundation, which is called a good work or law, even though no good work is there, but only wicked works, and no one does the Law (as Christ, John 7:19, says), but all transgress it. Therefore the building (that is raised upon it) is nothing but falsehood and hypocrisy, even (in the part) where it is most holy and beautiful.

And in Christians this repentance continues until death, because, through the entire life it contends with sin remaining in the flesh, as Paul, Rom. 7:14-25, (shows) testifies that he wars with the law in his members, etc.; and that, not by his own powers, but by the gift of the Holy Ghost that follows the remission of sins. This gift daily cleanses and sweeps out the remaining sins, and works so as to render man truly pure and holy.

The Pope, the theologians, the jurists, and every other man know nothing of this (from their own reason), but it is a doctrine from heaven, revealed through the Gospel, and must suffer to be called heresy by the godless saints (or hypocrites).

On the other hand, if certain sectarists would arise, some of whom are perhaps already extant, and in the time of the insurrection (of the peasants) came to my own view, holding that all those who had once received the Spirit or the forgiveness of sins, or had become believers, even though they should afterwards sin, would still remain in the faith, and such sin would not harm them, and (hence) crying thus: "Do whatever you please; if you believe, it all amounts to nothing; faith blots out all sins," etc.—they say, besides, that if any one sins after he has received faith and the Spirit, he never truly had the Spirit and faith: I have had before me (seen and heard) many such insane men, and I fear that in some such a devil is still remaining (hiding and dwelling).

It is, accordingly, necessary to know and to teach that when holy men, still having and feeling original sin, also daily repenting of and striving with it, happen to fall into manifest sins, as David into adultery, murder, and blasphemy, that then faith and the Holy Ghost has departed from them (they cast out faith and the Holy Ghost). For the Holy Ghost does not permit sin to have dominion, to gain the upper hand so as to be accomplished, but represses and restrains it so that it must not do what it wishes. But if it does what it wishes, the Holy Ghost and faith are (certainly) not present. For St. John says, 1 Jn. 3:9: Whosoever is born of God doth not commit sin,... and he cannot sin. And yet it is also the truth when the same St. John says, 1 Jn. 1:8: If we say that we have no sin, we deceive ourselves and the truth is not in us.

IV. Of the Gospel

We will now return to the Gospel, which not merely in one way gives us counsel and aid against sin; for God is superabundantly rich (and liberal) in His grace (and goodness). First, through the spoken Word by which the forgiveness of sins is preached (He commands to be preached) in the whole world; which is the peculiar office of the Gospel. Secondly, through Baptism. Thirdly, through the holy Sacrament of the Altar. Fourthly, through the power of the keys, and also through the mutual conversation and consolation of brethren, Matt. 18:20: Where two or three are gathered together, etc.

V. Of Baptism

Baptism is nothing else than the Word of God in the water, commanded by His institution, or, as Paul says, a washing in the Word; as also Augustine says: Let the Word come to the element, and it becomes a Sacrament. And for this reason we do not hold with Thomas and the monastic preachers (or Dominicans) who forget the Word (God's institution) and say that God has imparted to the water a spiritual power, which through the water washes away sin. Nor (do we agree) with Scotus and the Barefooted monks (Minorites or Franciscan monks), who teach that, by the assistance of the divine will, Baptism washes away sins, and that this ablution occurs only through the will of God, and by no means through the Word or water. Of the baptism of children we hold that children ought to be baptized. For they belong to the promised redemption made through Christ, and the Church should administer it (Baptism and the announcement of that promise) to them.

VI. Of the Sacrament of the Altar

Of the Sacrament of the Altar we hold that bread and wine in the Supper are the true body and blood of Christ, and are given and received not only by the godly, but also by wicked Christians.

And that not only one form is to be given. (For) we do not need that high art (specious wisdom) which is to teach us that under the one form there is as much as under both, as the sophists and the Council of Constance teach. For even if it were true that there is as much under one as under both, yet the one form only is not the entire ordinance and institution (made) ordained and commanded by Christ. And we especially condemn and in God's name execrate those who not only omit both forms but also quite autocratically (tyrannically) prohibit, condemn, and blaspheme them as heresy, and so exalt themselves against and above Christ, our Lord and God (opposing and placing themselves ahead of Christ), etc.

As regards transubstantiation, we care nothing about the sophistical subtlety by which they teach that bread and wine leave or lose their own natural substance, and that there remain only the appearance and color of bread, and not true bread. For it is in perfect agreement with Holy Scriptures that there is, and remains, bread, as Paul himself calls it, 1 Cor. 10:16: The bread which we break. And 1 Cor. 11:28: Let him so eat of that bread.

VII. Of the Keys

The keys are an office and power given by Christ to the Church for binding and loosing sin, not only the gross and well-known sins, but also the subtle, hidden, which are known only to God, as it is written in Ps. 19:13: Who can understand his errors? And in Rom. 7:25 St. Paul himself complains that with the flesh he serves the law of sin. For it is not in our power, but belongs to God alone, to judge which, how great, and how many the sins are, as it is written in Ps. 143:2: Enter not into judgment with Thy servant; for in Thy sight shall no man living be justified. And Paul, 1 Cor. 4:4, says: For I know nothing by myself; yet am I not hereby justified.

VIII. Of Confession

Since Absolution or the Power of the Keys is also an aid and consolation against sin and a bad conscience, ordained by Christ (Himself) in the Gospel, Confession or Absolution ought by no means to be abolished in the Church, especially on account of (tender and) timid consciences and on account of the untrained (and capricious) young people, in order that they may be examined, and instructed in the Christian doctrine.

But the enumeration of sins ought to be free to every one, as to what he wishes to enumerate or not to enumerate. For as long as we are in the flesh, we shall not lie when we say: "I am a poor man (I acknowledge that I am a miserable sinner), full of sin." Rom. 7:23: I see another law in my members, etc. For since private absolution originates in the Office of the Keys, it should not be despised (neglected), but greatly and highly esteemed (of the greatest worth), as (also) all other offices of the Christian Church.

And in those things which concern the spoken, outward Word, we must firmly hold that God grants His Spirit or grace to no one, except through or with the preceding outward Word, in order that we may (thus) be protected against the enthusiasts, i.e., spirits who boast that they have the Spirit without and before the Word, and accordingly judge Scripture or the spoken Word, and explain and stretch it at their pleasure, as Muenzer did, and many still do at the present day, who wish to be acute judges between the Spirit and the letter, and yet know not what they say or declare. For (indeed) the Papacy also is nothing but sheer enthusiasm, by which the Pope boasts that all rights exist in the shrine of his heart, and whatever he decides and commands with (in) his church is spirit and right, even though it is above and contrary to Scripture and the spoken Word.

All this is the old devil and old serpent, who also converted Adam and Eve into enthusiasts, and led them from the outward Word of God to spiritualizing and self-conceit, and nevertheless he accomplished this through other outward words. Just as also our enthusiasts (at the present day) condemn the outward Word, and nevertheless they themselves are not silent, but they fill the world with their pratings and writings, as though, indeed, the Spirit could not come through the writings and spoken word of the apostles, but (first) through their writings and words he must come. Why (then) do not they also omit their own sermons and writings, until the Spirit Himself come to men, without their writings and before them, as they boast that Me has come into them without the preaching of the Scriptures? But of these matters there is not time now to dispute at greater length; we have elsewhere sufficiently urged this subject.

For even those who believe before Baptism, or become believing in Baptism, believe through the preceding outward Word, as the adults, who have come to reason, must first have heard: He that believeth and is baptized shall be saved, even though they are at first unbelieving, and receive the Spirit and Baptism ten years afterwards. Cornelius, Acts 10:1 ff., had heard long before among the Jews of the coming Messiah, through whom he was righteous before God, and in such faith his prayers and alms were acceptable to God (as Luke calls him devout and God-fearing), and without such preceding Word and hearing could not have believed or been righteous. But St. Peter had to reveal to him that the Messiah (in whom, as one that was to come, he had hitherto believed) now had come, lest his faith concerning the coming Messiah hold him captive among the hardened and unbelieving Jews, but know that he was now to be saved by the present Messiah, and must not, with the (rabble of the) Jews deny nor persecute Him.

In a word, enthusiasm inheres in Adam and his children from the beginning (from the first fall) to the end of the world, (its poison) having been implanted and infused into them by the old dragon, and is the origin, power (life), and strength of all heresy, especially of that of the Papacy and Mahomet. Therefore we ought and must constantly maintain this point, that God does not wish to deal with us otherwise than through the spoken Word and the Sacraments. It is the devil himself whatsoever is extolled as Spirit without the Word and Sacraments. For God wished to appear even to Moses through the burning bush and spoken Word; and no prophet neither Elijah nor Elisha, received the Spirit without the Ten Commandments (or spoken Word). Neither was John the Baptist conceived without the preceding word of Gabriel, nor did he leap in his mother's womb without the voice of Mary. And Peter says, 2 Pet. 1:21: The prophecy came not by the will of man; but holy men of God spake as they were moved by the Holy Ghost. Without the outward Word, however, they were not holy, much less would the Holy Ghost have moved them to speak when they still were unholy (or profane); for they were holy, says he, since the Holy Ghost spake through them.

IX. Of Excommunication

The greater excommunication, as the Pope calls it, we regard only as a civil penalty, and it does not concern us ministers of the Church. But the lesser, that is, the true Christian excommunication, consists in this, that manifest and obstinate sinners are not admitted to the Sacrament and other communion of the Church until they amend their lives and avoid sin. And ministers ought not to mingle secular punishments with this ecclesiastical punishment, or excommunication.

X. Of Ordination and the Call

If the bishops would be true bishops (would rightly discharge their office), and would devote themselves to the Church and the Gospel, it might be granted to them for the sake of love and unity, but not from necessity, to ordain and confirm us and our preachers; omitting, however, all comedies and spectacular display (deceptions, absurdities, and appearances) of unchristian (heathenish) parade and pomp. But because they neither are, nor wish to be, true bishops, but worldly lords and princes, who will neither preach, nor teach, nor baptize, nor administer the Lord's Supper, nor perform any work or office of the Church, and, moreover, persecute and condemn those who discharge these functions, having been called to do so, the Church ought not on their account to remain without ministers (to be forsaken by or deprived of ministers).

Therefore, as the ancient examples of the Church and the Fathers teach us, we ourselves will and ought to ordain suitable persons to this office; and, even according to their own laws, they have not the right to forbid or prevent us. For their laws say that those ordained even by heretics should be declared (truly) ordained and stay ordained (and that such ordination must not be changed), as St. Jerome writes of the Church at Alexandria, that at first it was governed in common by priests and preachers, without bishops.

XI. Of the Marriage of Priests

To prohibit marriage, and to burden the divine order of priests with perpetual celibacy, they have had neither authority nor right (they have done out of malice, without any honest reason), but have acted like antichristian, tyrannical, desperate scoundrels (have performed the work of antichrist, of tyrants and the worst knaves), and have thereby caused all kinds of horrible, abominable, innumerable sins of unchastity (depraved lusts), in which they still wallow. Now, as little as we or they have been given the power to make a woman out of a man or a man out of a woman, or to nullify either sex, so little have they had the power to (sunder and) separate such creatures of God, or to forbid them from living (and cohabiting) honestly in marriage with one another. Therefore we are unwilling to assent to their abominable celibacy, nor will we (even) tolerate it, but we wish to have marriage free as God has instituted (and ordained) it, and we wish neither to rescind nor hinder His work; for Paul says, 1 Tim. 4:1 ff., that this (prohibition of marriage) is a doctrine of devils.

XII. Of the Church

We do not concede to them that they are the Church, and (in truth) they are not (the Church); nor will we listen to those things which, under the name of Church, they enjoin or forbid. For, thank God, (today) a child seven years old knows what the Church is, namely, the holy believers and lambs who hear the voice of their Shepherd. For the children pray thus: I believe in one holy (catholic or) Christian Church. This holiness does not consist in albs, tonsures, long gowns, and other of their ceremonies devised by them beyond Holy Scripture, but in the Word of God and true faith.

XIII. How One is Justified before God, and of Good Works

What I have hitherto and constantly taught concerning this I know not how to change in the least, namely, that by faith, as St. Peter says, we acquire a new and clean heart, and God will and does account us entirely righteous and holy for the sake of Christ, our Mediator. And although sin in the flesh has not yet been altogether removed or become dead, yet He will not punish or remember it.

And such faith, renewal, and forgiveness of sins is followed by good works. And what there is still sinful or imperfect also in them shall not be accounted as sin or defect, even (and that, too) for Christ's sake; but the entire man, both as to his person and his works, is to be called and to be righteous and holy from pure grace and mercy, shed upon us (unfolded) and spread over us in Christ. Therefore we cannot boast of many merits and works, if they are viewed apart from grace and mercy, but as it is written, 1 Cor. 1:31: He that glorieth, let him glory in the Lord, namely, that he has a gracious God. For thus all is well. We say, besides, that if good works do not follow, faith is false and not true.

XIV. Of Monastic Vows

As monastic vows directly conflict with the first chief article, they must be absolutely abolished. For it is of them that Christ says, Matt. 24:5 (23 ff.): I am Christ, etc. For he who makes a vow to live as a monk believes that he will enter upon a mode of life holier than ordinary Christians lead, and wishes to earn heaven by his own works not only for himself, but also for others; this is to deny Christ. And they boast from their St. Thomas that a monastic vow is equal to Baptism. This is blasphemy (against God).

XV. Of Human Traditions

The declaration of the Papists that human traditions serve for the remission of sins, or merit salvation, is (altogether) unchristian and condemned, as Christ says Matt. 15:9: In vain they do worship Me, teaching for doctrines the commandments of men. Again, Titus 1:14: That turn from the truth. Again, when they declare that it is a mortal sin if one breaks these ordinances (does not keep these statutes), this, too, is not right.

These are the articles on which I must stand, and, God willing, shall stand even to my death; and I do not know how to change or to yield anything in them. If any one wishes to yield anything, let him do it at the peril of his conscience.

Lastly, there still remains the Pope's bag of impostures concerning foolish and childish articles, as, the dedication of churches, the baptism of bells, the baptism of the altarstone, and the inviting of sponsors to these rites, who would make donations towards them.

Such baptizing is a reproach and mockery of Holy Baptism, hence should not be tolerated. Furthermore, concerning the consecration of wax-tapers, palm-branches, cakes, oats, (herbs,) spices, etc., which indeed, cannot be called consecrations, but are sheer mockery and fraud. And such deceptions there are without number, which we commend for adoration to their god and to themselves, until they weary of it. We will (ought to) have nothing to do with them.

Dr. Martin Luther subscribed.

Dr. Justus Jonas, Rector, subscribed with his own hand.

Dr. John Bugenhagen, Pomeranus, subscribed.

Dr. Caspar Creutziger subscribed.

Nicholas Amsdorf of Magdeburg subscribed.

George Spalatin of Altenburg subscribed.

I, Philip Melanchthon, also regard (approve) the above articles as right and Christian. But regarding the Pope I hold that, if he would allow the Gospel, his superiority over the bishops which he has otherwise, is conceded to him by human right also by us, for the sake of the peace and general unity of those Christians who are also under him, and may be under him hereafter.

John Agricola of Eisleben subscribed. Gabriel Didymus subscribed.

I, Dr. Urban Rhegius, Superintendent of the churches in the Duchy of Lueneburg, subscribe in my own name and in the name of my brethren, and of the Church of Hanover.

I, Stephen Agricola, Minister at Hof, subscribe.

Also I, John Draconites, Professor and Minister at Marburg, subscribe.

I, Conrad Figenbotz, for the glory of God subscribe that I have thus believed, and am still preaching and firmly believing as above.

I, Andrew Osiander of Nuernberg, subscribe. I, Magister Veit Dieterich, Minister at Nuernberg, subscribe.

I, Erhard Schnepf, Preacher at Stuttgart, subscribe. Conrad Oettinger, Preacher of Duke Ulrich at Pforzheim. Simon Schneeweiss, Pastor of the Church at Crailsheim.

I, John Schlagenhaufen, Pastor of the Church at Koethen, subscribe.

The Reverend Magister George Helt of Forchheim. The R

verend Magister Adam of Fulda, Preacher in Hesse. The Reverend Magister Anthony Corvinus, Preacher in Hesse.

I, Doctor John Bugenhagen, Pomeranus, again subscribe in the name of Magister John Brentz, as on departing from Smalcald he directed me orally and by a letter, which I have shown to these brethren who have subscribed.

I, Dionysius Melander, subscribe to the Confession, the Apology, and the Concordia on the subject of the Eucharist.

Paul Rhodius, Superintendent of Stettin. Gerard Oemcken, Superintendent of the Church at Minden.

I, Brixius Northanus, Minister of the Church of Christ which is at Soest, subscribe to the Articles of the Reverend Father Martin Luther, and confess that hitherto I have thus believed and taught, and by the Spirit of Christ I shall continue thus to believe and teach.

Michael Caelius, Preacher at Mansfeld, subscribed. The Reverend Magister Peter Geltner Preacher at Frankfort, subscribed. Wendal Faber, Pastor of Seeburg in Mansfeld.

I, John Aepinus, subscribe. Likewise, I, John Amsterdam of Bremen.

I, Frederick Myconius, Pastor of the Church at Gotha in Thuringia, subscribe in my own name and in that of Justus Menius of Eisenach.

I, Doctor John Lang, Preacher of the Church at Erfurt, subscribe with my own hand in my own name, and in that of my other coworkers in the Gospel, namely: The Reverend Licentiate Ludwig Platz of Melsungen. The Reverend Magister Sigismund Kirchner, The Reverend Wolfgang Kiswetter, The Reverend Melchior Weitmann The Reverend John Thall. The Reverend John Kilian. The Reverend Nicholas Faber. The Reverend Andrew Menser.

And I, Egidius Mechler, have subscribed with my own hand.

THE MISSION OF GREAT CHRISTIAN BOOKS

The ministry of Great Christian Books was established to glorify The Lord Jesus Christ and to be used by Him to expand and edify the kingdom of God while we occupy and anticipate Christ's glorious return. Great Christian Books will seek to accomplish this mission by publishing Gospel literature which is biblically faithful, relevant, and practically applicable to many of the serious spiritual needs of mankind upon the beginning of this new millennium. To do so we will always seek to boldly incorporate the truths of Scripture, especially those which were largely articulated as a body of theology during the Protestant Reformation of the sixteenth century and ensuing years. We gladly join our voice in the proclamations of— Scripture Alone, Faith Alone, Grace Alone, Christ Alone, and God's Glory Alone!

Our ministry seeks the blessing of our God as we seek His face to both confirm and support our labors for Him. Our prayers for this work can be summarized by two verses from the Book of Psalms:

> "...let the beauty of the LORD our God be upon us, And establish the work of our hands for us; Yes, establish the work of our hands." —Psalm 90:17

> "Not unto us, O LORD, not unto us, but to your name give glory." —Psalm 115:1

Great Christian Books appreciates the financial support of anyone who shares our burden and vision for publishing literature which combines sound Bible doctrine and practical exhortation in an age when too few so-called "Christian" publications do the same. We thank you in advance for any assistance you can give us in our labors to fulfill this important mission. May God bless you.

For a catalog of other great
Christian books
contact us in
any of the following ways:

write us at:
Great Christian Books
160 37th Street
Lindenhurst, NY 11757

call us at:
631. 956. 0998

find us online:
www.greatchristianbooks.com

email us at:
mail@greatchristianbooks.com